Carving Songbird Ornaments with Power

Frank C. Russell

Schiffer Publishing Ltd

4880 Lower Valley Road, Atglen, Pennsylvania 19310

Dedication

To Caroline, my bride of 50 years –

for all she has done for me,
for all she has been to me,
for all she means to me.

Cover design by Frank C. Russell

Other Schiffer Books by Frank C. Russell
Carving Animal Canes & Walking Sticks with Power. ISBN: 0764323814.
$14.95.
*Carving Patterns by Frank C. Russell: from the Stonegate Woodcarving
School: Birds, Animals, Fish.* ISBN: 076432473X. $14.95.
Carving Realistic Animals with Power. ISBN: 0887406378. $12.95.
Carving Realistic Faces with Power. ISBN: 0887404863. $12.95.
Carving Wildfowl Canes and Walking Sticks with Power. ISBN:
0764315897. $14.95

Other Schiffer Books on Related Subjects
Favorite Songbirds. Roger S. Everett. ISBN: 0887401511. $12.95.
Powercarving Birds, Fish and Penguins: Using Beautiful Hardwoods.
Gene Larson. ISBN: 0887405657. $12.95.

Designed by Mark David Bowyer
Type set in Americana XBd BT / Zurich BT

ISBN: 978-0-7643-3135-0
Printed in China

Schiffer Books are available at special discounts for bulk purchases for
sales promotions or premiums. Special editions, including personalized
covers, corporate imprints, and excerpts can be created in large quanti-
ties for special needs. For more information contact the publisher:

Published by Schiffer Publishing Ltd.
4880 Lower Valley Road
Atglen, PA 19310
Phone: (610) 593-1777; Fax: (610) 593-2002
E-mail: Info@schifferbooks.com

Please visit our web site catalog at
www.schifferbooks.com

We are always looking for people to write
books on new and related subjects.
If you have an idea for a book,
please contact us at the above address.

This book may be purchased from the publisher.
Include $5.00 for shipping.
Please try your bookstore first.
You may write for a free catalog.

In Europe, Schiffer books are distributed by:
Bushwood Books
6 Marksbury Ave.
Kew Gardens
Surrey TW9 4JF
England
Phone: 44 (0)208 392-8585
Fax: 44 (0)208 392-9876
E-mail: Info@bushwoodbooks.co.uk

Website: www.bushwoodbooks.co.uk
Free postage in the UK. Europe: air mail at cost.
Try your bookstore first.

Contents

Introduction

This book was prompted by the hundreds of queries received in response to an article I wrote featuring the chickadee ornament whose working drawings and finished photo are displayed in this book. The requests were primarily for songbirds similar to the chickadee ornament. Most woodcarvers who wrote wanted to carve a heritage series for themselves or as Christmas gifts for relatives and friends.

All but a few were primarily interested in the patterns and carving aspects of such projects, as opposed to the application of color. There were so many preferences and already acquired methods of applying color, that I decided to dedicate my efforts primarily to the carving of the projects and only touch briefly on *my* method of painting. To field the diverse requests relating to acrylics, oils, and watercolors from manual brush to airbrush application would have gone far beyond the intended scope of this book; however, such requests have created a well-defined path for future writing.

Choice of Carving Woods

I paint virtually everything I carve, and because Tupelo is so forgiving and accepts the highest degree of detail for power carving, I have used this wood for every project featured in this book. Depending on choice of tools and level of detail, however, woods such as basswood, cedar, pine, poplar, etc. are all also quite suitable choices. If a natural finish is desired, choose a wood that offers both color and grain, such as cherry, walnut, butternut or a colorful species of exotic wood.

The sequences necessary to carve a Red-breasted Nuthatch are shown as the follow-through project. The basic information given in the text and shown pictorially with each sequence step through to the completion of the carving is essentially the same for every pattern/project in this book. So, once you accomplish the first carving project to your satisfaction, any one you choose to carve from that point on should be much easier.

Any bird I carve will always have the same format when it comes to finish texturing the feathers, in that all flight feathers (those hard looking feathers that sustain flight), such as the primary wing feathers, the secondary feathers, tertials, scapulars, and tail feathers are always textured by wood burning. Wood burning gives a harder appearing surface to those stiffer flight feathers as they appear on a real bird.

The desired effect for contour feathers (those feathers that provide warmth and protection), such as head, chest, cape, back, flank, and tail coverts, requires a softer look. The softest textured look for these feathers is accomplished by texturing with a stone bit.

Both techniques for texturing are covered more completely later in this book.

Dust Control

The first consideration for safety for any power carving or sanding operation is control of the dust that is generated. Remember! It isn't the dust that we can see that should be feared and guarded against – it's the air-borne dust that cannot be seen that should be feared and given the greatest preventative measure. Without preventive care, this airborne dust is inhaled and taken into the lungs. In the lungs this dust is held fast and will eventually create dire medical problems.

I learned the hard way some twenty years ago when I ended up in the hospital with what were thought to be cancer spots on my lungs. A biopsy showed that they were not cancerous, but large clumps of ingested dust that I had inhaled over a prolonged period of time while carving, and the lungs had forced that dust into clumps while trying to cleanse themselves.

Unfortunately, power carving precludes carving in any convenient place that we wish to carve – such as in our living rooms, dens, or game rooms in front of the television. I learned early from my bride (now my bride of 50 years) that power carving in the house was a greater sin than throwing my hip boots and fishing gear in a convenient corner after a return from the wilds…now that I remember it, cleaning fish in the bathroom also qualified as a misdemeanor.

I will consider at least three areas here that have to be addressed in regards to cleanliness and safety involving dust control in each of my three studios:

The first and foremost is the dust collection system directly attached to my carving station.

For my school in Vermont, this system consisted of an inlet hole for each of the 16 carving stations with a blast gate (a blast gate allows that particular station to be closed when not in use or opened for use) where the dust that was directed into the intake holes was carried to a commercial dust collecting unit housed in a separate room. This separate room was insulated and not only localized what dust was collected but kept noise to an absolute minimum in the classroom.

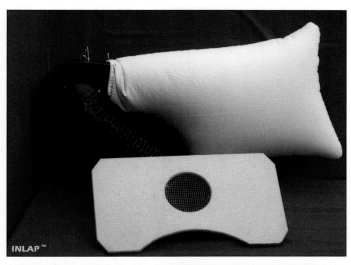

INLAP™

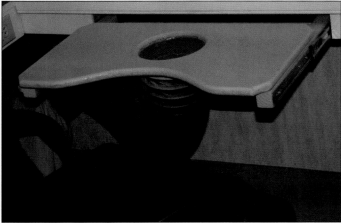

For my studios in Florida and at my camp on the lake, I have an In-lap® dust collector that has its own motor/fan and collection bag. These units can be used by holding the collection board on your lap, or, to save space in my two smaller studios, I have built them directly under the bench attached to drawer tracks so the lapboard can be pushed out of the way under the bench top. The lapboards are attached to the drawer rails with wing nuts that allow for easy removal if I choose to use the unit at a woodcarving show, demonstration, or seminar that I am teaching. Extremely quiet and powerful, without a bothersome flat filter to deal with and constantly clean, each unit features a removable, reusable bag that can be emptied periodically.

Every time I empty the collection bags (GENTLY in a garbage bag or a nearby empty barrel or you will have dust all over the place), I turn the bag inside-out and slap it against a bush in the back yard, then I ask my wife to wash it. (I don't do beds or washing machines!) With the size of the items that I have been carving in either of my studios, I don't have to clean the bags more often than every 4 or 5 months.

The lapboard is connected to the motor and collection bag by a length of 6-inch flexible tubing which allows for countless mounting configurations under or beside a workbench or table. I have yet to find a more efficient or mobile dust collector that can also be used as a permanent fixture.

For additional product information, contact: In-Lap Dust Collection Systems, Inc., Box 081576, Racine, WI 53408-1576; Ph: 262-633-8899.

The next area I address is the dust-laden air that is unseen for the most part and can permeate the entire studio area. For this, at my school studio, I have mounted two filtered fan boxes on the ceiling on either side of the room, with each facing in an opposite direction from the other. I feel that this creates a circular movement to the air with the "current" being drawn into the filtered intake of the boxes. Before using these filter boxes, the entire studio would be covered with a fine, powder-like dust.

The final area that I concentrate on is the immediate area around me from which I breathe. I wear a dust mask rated for minuscule particle filtration at any time I am generating dust, and most especially when I am generating fine dust, such as during finish shaping or texturing. I steer clear of the "cheapy" dust masks, and also dislike the large rubber over nose and mouth types. There are several with heavy-duty filter material, heavy elastic bands to hold them in place, and outflow valves that direct the breath through the valve as it is exhaled – preventing eye glasses from fogging.

One of my favorite particulate respirator masks of this type is the Moldex® #2731 – this Moldex brand also has many other dust mask options and configurations for woodcarvers to choose from. To view the complete line of disposable dust masks, log on to **www.moldex.com**.

Carving Equipment and Accessories

Flexible Shaft Machine

My preference for the roughing out and primary shaping of any carving that I do is a flexible shaft machine. The unit used for roughing every project in this book was the Foredom® SR flexible shaft machine. There are many other similar and suitable machines of this type on the market, but my preference has always been for this particular model and company because I began carving with it, and later set up every position at my school with the same model. I have enjoyed the longevity, durability, simplicity of repair, and ease of obtaining parts (rarely necessary) for this machine or any of the Foredom® line of tools and accessories.

The "S" model Foredom flexible shaft machine runs at a maximum 1800 rpm (revolutions per minute) and generates one-sixth horsepower. The "S" in the SR machine indicator denotes the model, and the "R" indicates that it has a reverse – a necessity if you are a left-handed power carver. Lefthanders have to run their machines in reverse in order to maintain the same control that a right-hander has with a machine running forward. To better understand this, if you are right-handed, put your machine in reverse and try to carve with it – notice how the carving stroke tries to "run away" from you. The lefthander gets the same feeling with a machine that runs in the conventional "forward" manner.

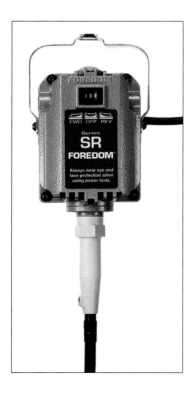

Handpieces

A large and small handpiece was used for the initial roughing and shaping on each of the projects in this book. The large handpiece (Foredom handpiece #44) was used for begin "hogging" – the removal of waste wood and preliminary rough shaping. The small handpiece (Foredom handpiece #28) was used to refine shapes.

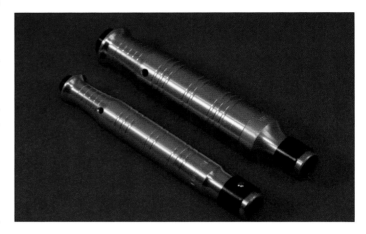

The flexible shaft machine can certainly be used throughout the entirety of the carvings, but once I have accomplished rough shaping to a point that replicates the bird I am creating, I switch to the Micro motor machine to perform the finish shaping and texturing operations, as will be described under the Micro motor machine description that follows.

Machine Hanger

The machine hanger is a device for suspending a flexible shaft machine where it is easily accessible, yet out of the way of the carving process. Hangers are available commercially as permanently attached bench top models, or clamp-on models that allow the hanger to be moved from place to place. I keep my clamp-on hanger in a travel box just for when I demonstrate at shows, do lectures, or go to a carving club meeting to carve with my friends.

An easily constructed home-made clamp-on hanger uses a 4-inch C-clamp bolted to one end of

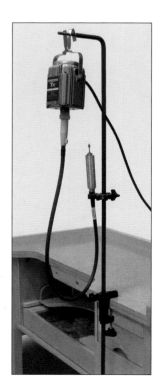

a 32-inch piece of metal conduit, with an eyebolt (with the eye pried open) bolted through a hole at the other end.

Micro Motor

The reasons I switch to a micro motor machine after roughing out with the flexible shaft machine are for ease of finish carving and detailing. I find the micro motor-type machines offer greater freedom of movement, as one is not "tethered" by a large fixed length shaft. Unlike the "drag" and general restriction in maneuverability encountered with a shaft and sheath machine, micro motors offer much greater freedom of movement. The cord connecting the handpiece to the control box allows for a more unrestricted movement about the surface of the carving, which ultimately makes for greater ease in creating detail and without hand/wrist fatigue.

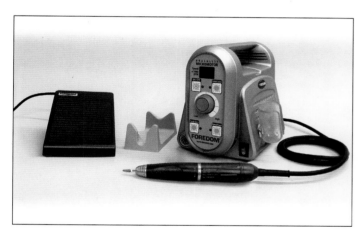

Compared to flex shafts, micro motors have much less torque, but the higher speeds serve several other very important purposes. First, the higher the rpm, the smoother the cut – a blessing when finish shaping and/or texturing feathers. Secondly, the Micro motor delivers a comparable rate of material removal to the flexible shaft machine, but with a lighter touch.

This is not to say that a micro motor can be used to waste away large amounts of stock. The wasting away and rough shaping are functions of the flexible shaft machine with it's rating of 1/6th horsepower, and the finesse finishing functions (refined shaping, detailing, and texturing) are left to the micro motor machine with around 1/100th horsepower.

Bit Holders

Rotating bit holders are of absolute necessity for categorizing and locating the countless bits I own. I need several of the rotating holders just to contain the assorted sizes and types.

Note: A rotating bit holder with 1/8-inch holes will also hold wood burning pens because the connectors on the end of the pens fit into the holes perfectly.

To keep from having to search through a large selection of bits in a rotating bit holder each time you have a bit change or need to return to a bit previously used, take the magnet out of an old speaker and set it within easy reach. Each time you need to use a bit for repeated operations, it is easier to pluck the needed bit off a 1 1/2-inch magnet than to search for the same bit time after time by spinning a rotating bit holder back and forth. I mention the 1 1/2-inch size because a larger magnet is too powerful – I had a 4-inch diameter magnet that I thought would be wonderful, only to find that it not only took two hands to retrieve a bit, but it magnetized some of the bits in the process.

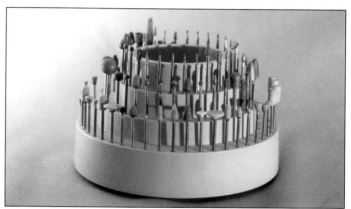

With the exception of the magnet bit holder from a speaker, shown above, the flexible shaft, micro motor, bits, rotating bit holder, and other accessories are available from: Foredom Electric Company, 16 Stony Hill Road, Bethel, CT 06801, and can be seen on their website at **www.foredom.com**.

Woodcarving Bits

Every bit used for the size of projects in this book is pictured, physically described, and how it was used with regard to these projects. Where appropriate, a thumbnail photo will also be included with the appropriate sequence photo to assist with the various carving sequences. *Note: where two bits are pictured together, either can be used for the same operation. Bit head sizes are given as head diameter x head length.*

Carbide bit, flame shape, large size – 1/4-shaft, 5/8" x 1 1/16" head, coarse grit.
Use: Initial wasting away (hogging) and rough shaping the carving blanks.

Carbide bit, flame shape, small size – 3/32-inch shaft, 5/16" x 1/2" head, fine grit.
Use: Minute wasting away and defining rough shapes.

Carbide bit, flame shape, medium size – 1/8-shaft, 5/16" x 3/4" head, coarse grit.
Use: Initial wasting away (hogging) and rough shaping the carving blanks.

Ruby bit, flame shape, large size – 3/32" shaft, 6.5mm x 12mm head, medium grit.
Use: Refining shapes and smoothing.

Ruby bit, flame shape, medium size – 3/32" shaft, 3.3mm x 8mm head, medium grit.
   Use: Defining shapes, detailing shape, and minimal smoothing.

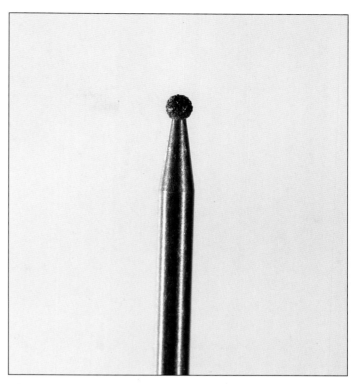

Diamond bit, ball shape, small size – 3/32" shaft, 2.1mm head, coarse grit.
   Use: Outlining feathers in step one of contour feather relieving.

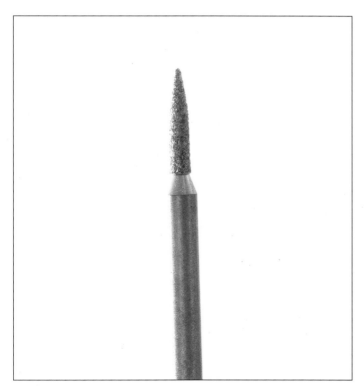

Diamond bit, flame shape, small size – 3/32" shaft, 1.6mm x 9mm head, medium grit.
   Use: Outlining, shaping, and detailing a carved eye.

Ruby bit, ball shape, medium size – 3/32" shaft, 4.5mm head, medium grit.
   Use: Carving out and sizing eye cavities in preparation for installing glass eyes.

(Right) Steel bit, tapered shape, small size – 3/32" shaft, 4mm x 9mm head, medium flute.
(Left) Ceramic stone, flame shape, small size – 3/32" shaft, 3.9mm x 9.5mm head, coarse grit.

(Right) Use: Relieving feathers in step two of contour feather relieving.

(Left) Use: Rounding and blending feathers one into the other in step three of contour feather relieving.

(Right) Ceramic stone, inverted cone shape, small size – 3/32" shaft, 3.2mm x 3.2mm head, fine grit.
(Left) Ceramic stone, cylinder shape, small size – 3/32" shaft, 2.35mm x 6.4mm head, fine grit.

Use: Texturing contour feathers and detailing the edges of some feather groups.

Rotary bristle brush, 2-inch diameter – 1/8" shaft.
Use: Cleaning both stone textured and wood burned textured surfaces.

Woodburning Pens and Control Unit

The woodburning control unit that I use is physically a small boxed unit, but it has all the power necessary to deliver an even current at any setting I choose with just about any woodburning pen from high resistance tips that I have built (such as large fish scale tips) to commercially manufactured tips that require much less current than the homemade silver soldered beauties that I create.

The woodburning control unit shown here is available from: PJL Enterprises, PO Box 273, 720 N. Perry Ave., Browerville, MN 56438 or on their website **www.carvertools.com**.

Before you begin outlining and texturing feathers with a woodburning pen, please review "Feather Texturing Guidelines".

All the feather outlining and texturing for the projects in this book was accomplished with just two woodburning pen tips – namely, a blunt bent skew tip and a straight sharp skew tip.

Bird Nomenclature & General Techniques

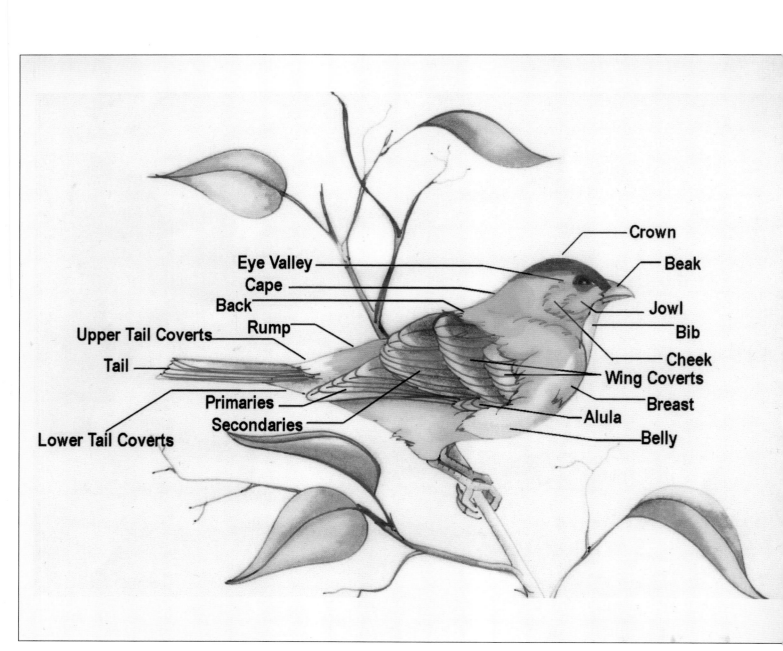

Crown

Eye Valley

Beak

Cape

Back

Jowl

Upper Tail Coverts

Rump

Bib

Tail

Cheek

Wing Coverts

Primaries

Breast

Secondaries

Alula

Lower Tail Coverts

Belly

Feather Parts

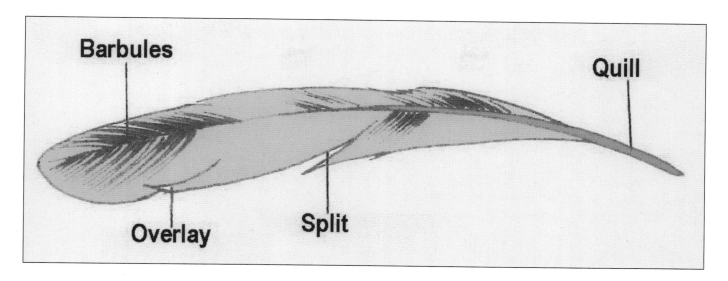

The above sketch shows the feather parts that will be dealt with for the feathers textured on the projects in this book.

The *quills* are visible on only a few feathers where a feather is either fully exposed such as the top feather in the tertials, or on exposed tips such as some of the primaries. When the quills **are** exposed, it is imperative that they be represented in proper length, size, and shape. The quill tapers to a sharp point before terminating at the end of the feather – it does not run all the way to the tip of the feather.

The *barbules* are those thin rays that run out from the feather to form the feather shape – and are of primary interest when we texture. If you note on a real feather, the barbules run equally parallel and do not vary in any way unless they *split* apart occasionally. An occasional split is acceptable and usually appealing, but too many splits look unnatural because a bird will usually preen before it accumulates too many feather splits. At times, a split will reverse into an *overlay*, which although not as common as a split, can add attraction to a carving.

Feather Types

Virtually every songbird has two major feather types – *contour* feathers and *flight* feathers – each type with a different sort of feather.

First are the contour feathers, those soft looking feathers that cover the head, breast, belly, flanks, back, under-tail, etc. These are the feathers that primarily provide warmth, protection, and shape to an individual bird.

Secondly are the flight feathers, the hard looking feathers such as the wing primaries, wing secondaries, tail feathers, tertials, and some scapulars that sustain flight, balance, and provide maneuverability for the bird.

Feather Groups

Both feather types (contour and flight) are broken into distinctive groups – each of which is dealt with on an individual basis while carving. Although each feather group is roughed, finish shaped, and detailed in much the same manner, the **contour** feather barbules (the lines representing the feather barbules that run out from the center quills) are textured by grinding with a stone bit, which gives a "soft" look to a feather, and the **flight** feather barbules are textured with a woodburning pen, which gives each feather a "hard" appearance.

Refer to the feather groups on the bird nomenclature sketch and the pattern drawings. Note the shape of the individual groups, as well as any companion group that exists on one side or the other of the bird.

Each of these groups will be relieved away and shaped to receive individual feathers. *A more complete understanding of the feather group carving process can be seen in the "Carving the Nuthatch" sequence.*

Feather Layout

On every bird, each feather group has, not only a certain size and shape of feathers, but a "flow" or direction. An example of this "flow" or direction can be found by observing how the feather groups join together or overlap, and how they flow to follow the curvature along the body or even away from it. An example of this might be the direction feathers take from under a bird's beak down the neck, through the breast feathers, along the belly, and through the under-tail coverts to the tail.

On your references, note how feathers join together to form a flow pattern that follows the curvature of the bird's body (such as the flow line created by the feathers that cover the lower neck, breast, belly, and lower tail coverts of a chickadee).

Giving life and a line of flow to the feathers on a carving is established *as* the feathers are drawn on the carving in preparation to shaping and texturing individual feathers. The indicators (flow lines) that are **drawn** are followed to the completion of the feather.

For the projects in this book, variations of a "clamshell" shape and/or a broadly pointed shape will do very well for drawing, shaping, and texturing *contour* feathers.

add that all feathers within a group do not have to be exactly the same size. Just like hairs on an animal or hairs on a human head, single feathers within a group are always being shed/broken and are replaced by new feather growth where the feather(s) have not reached full size. However, safety and appearance lies with drawing the vast majority of feathers within the group as nearly the same size as you can. Beware of drawing shingled, uniformly shaped feathers in even rows that give the appearance of roofing shingles – you are carving a songbird, not the roof on a house.

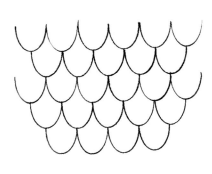

Once the feather outlines are drawn, draw "flow" lines within each feather to give direction to individual feathers which in turn will give direction to the feather group as a whole. *Compare the feathers drawn in figure 2 to the feathers drawn in figure 3. Figure 2 flow lines have direction, while Figure 3 flow lines are straight within the feather giving the feathers a stiff, no-life, non-directional look.*

Note the size and shape of the feathers over the entirety of a songbird – starting at the base of the bill, they are tiny and almost hair-like, get gradually larger to the middle body of the bird, then get somewhat smaller as they run into the tail coverts.

Draw the feathers and feather layout as you want them within each feather group.

You may find this somewhat difficult to get the result you want to begin with. If so, practice drawing feathers on paper until you can draw each feather with a single uniform stroke. Draw the curvature of each feather not only to shape, but to a size that matches the feathers within the group. I hasten to

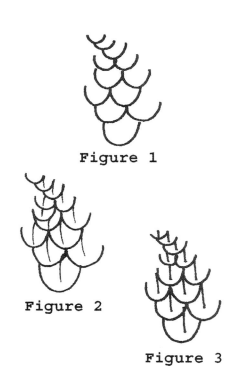

Figure 1

Figure 2

Figure 3

Shaping Individual Feathers

Once the feathers are drawn, to relieve away individual feathers within a contour feather group, two different bits are used to shape the individual feathers...a diamond ball bit and a fluted, tapered steel bit. Once the feathers are drawn to include any separation details as described in steps 2 through 5 that follow, there are three distinctive steps to shaping each individual feather.

1. Draw all feathers on the carving to the desired shape and size. Hold the carving at arm's length – if the feathers do not appear in the desired shape/ size, or don't appear to match the feathers on the rest of the carving, erase and redraw them until they are uniform, and you are satisfied with them.

2. As you hold the carving at arm's length, note areas where small groups of feathers *align* and appear suitable to relieving/separating away from the field, and draw a dark line along the edges where you will want them to separate away.

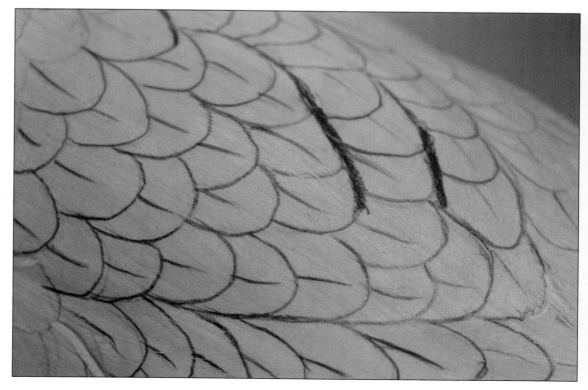

3. Using a small flame shaped ruby carver, drag the bit along these heavy lines at a fairly sharp angle that leaves a "V" bottomed cut at the depth you want. Make sure these cuts are not of so great a depth that the separation looks unrealistic.

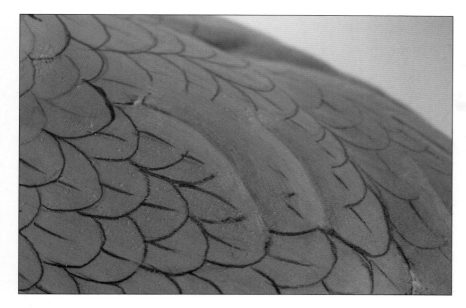

4. With the same small flame shaped ruby carver, round the sides of the outlined feather group to blend into the existing surfaces, or to form a rounded ridge from which raised feathers will be relieved away.

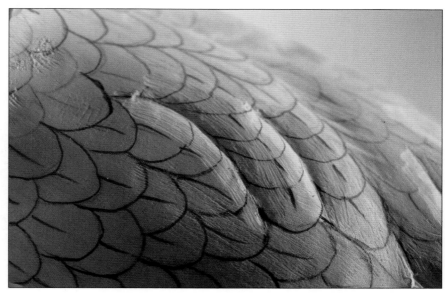

5. Redraw feathers in all the areas where the penciled outlines have been carved away. Take this opportunity to add additional feathers if needs be, enlarge or reduce feather sizes, or reposition some of the newly drawn feathers.

6. Step One: Begin the "three step feather shaping" process by holding the handpiece at about the same angle as you would hold a pen or pencil while writing, and outline each feather edge with a diamond ball bit of a size that is appropriate to the size of the feathers you are relieving away. Insure that each feather is outlined without leaving too large an outline groove for the size of the feather. Note: A ball bit is sometimes called a writing bit because of the ease it affords with respect to movement in any direction, in the same manner as a ballpoint pen.

7. Step Two: Holding the handpiece with the side of the steel tapered bit at an angle that matches the flattened surface of the top of the feather where it emerges from under the feather above it, shape the top of the feather from side to side, honoring the depth of the groove created with the ball bit while outlining the feather in Step One. A flame-shaped stone bit may be used for finished shaping and smoothing.

8. Step Three: Finish shape each feather using a wiping stroke on the exposed edge of each feather with the side of the steel tapered bit by "rolling" the exposed surface onto the feather below the feather being shaped. The finished shape of these rounded feathers will be reminiscent of a clamshell – laying one atop the other in a shingled fashion. Check the entire feather group for any misshapen or non-uniform feathers and correct them.

Feather Texturing Guidelines

☐ Use references – these days my first choice, for both reference photos for birds and scene/diorama ideas, is the Internet... A few minutes of searching usually gives me feather detail, color scheme, shape, and/or position for virtually anything I propose to carve, whether it be bird or animal. I also use the reference book photos and photo/detail folders that I have compiled, collected, and kept over the years. I have always worked on the premise that *you can't carve what you don't know.*

☐ Draw flow lines on individual feathers – flow lines give you a "feel", not only for how an individual feather lies directionally within a group, but the direction of the feather group as a whole. Flow lines are constant reference points to follow throughout the texturing process.

☐ Use an inverted cone or a cylinder shaped texturing stone – depending on the size of bird and scale of feather; you will want to consider the size of head and aggressiveness of the grit on the stone you are using. The choice for texture on the breast feathers of a chickadee would require a fine gritted stone with a 1/8-inch head or smaller, whereas the under-tail coverts of a red-tail hawk would warrant a stone with a larger, coarser head.

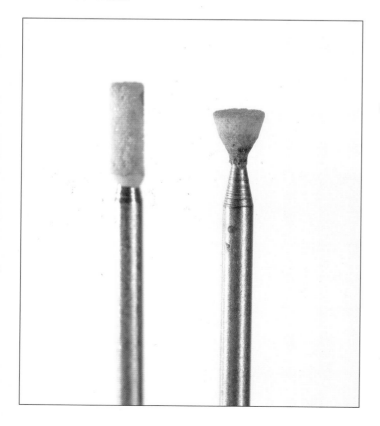

☐ Use a high speed for texturing – the higher the speed, the smoother the cut. The texturing process is one area where a micro motor machine is of necessity for two reasons:

First, the micro motor machine delivers a very high rate of RPMs (revolutions per minute) – depending on the manufacturer, these machines deliver in the range of 35,000 to 50,000 rpms, speeds that provide a very smooth cut. The flexible shaft machines, on the other hand, run at slower rpms and, depending on the manufacturer, only deliver from 17,000 to 20,000 rpms. Lower speeds don't provide as smooth a cut as do the higher speeds.

Secondly, the handpiece on a micro motor machine is much easier to use for the texturing operation. It provides greater freedom of movement with greater ease for making short back-and-forth texturing strokes than does a flexible shaft machine. The handpiece of the flexible shaft machine keeps the user "tethered" to the whole machine due to its make-up – *handpiece* to *shaft and sheath* to *motor* to *hanger*. Because of its power, it is a wonderful machine for roughing out, shaping, and some detailing. But when it comes to the prolonged, repetitive stroking required by texturing, the "tether" effect creates hand/wrist fatigue, along with arm and shoulder discomfort. Having stated all this, the flexible shaft was all I had to work with when I first started carving, so I *made* it work. However, once I was introduced to the quality, speed, freedom, ease of texturing, and fine detailing with a micro motor machine, I added one as a permanent part of my carving war chest.

Texturing Hints (Stone or Burner Texturing)

☐ Start from the bottom feathers and work up

☐ Start from the rear feathers in a group and work forward

☐ Follow the direction of the flow lines

☐ Back and forth strokes (as opposed to uni-directional strokes)

☐ Keep strokes close together (no flats between the "V"s that the bit cuts)

☐ Vary the size of feathers on layout

☐ Beware of "shingling"

☐ Roll feather edges (there are no square or hard feather edges)

☐ Relieve and/or shape all feathers before texturing

☐ - See Three Step Feather Shaping and Relief

☐ - See Feather Relief with a Woodburner
☐ Burning: too hot/too cool (establish heat setting before texturing carving)
☐ Clean all texturing thoroughly with a soft brush

Note: The majority of the hints mentioned above are clarified in the text accompanying the texturing sequences.

Feather Texturing with a Stone Bit

Once the individual contour feathers are formed, they are textured with lines to resemble the feather barbules on a natural feather. This is accomplished by single stroking or double stroking the feather shape with either a cylinder shaped stone bit or an inverted cone shaped stone bit.

The top edge of either a cylinder or cone shaped stone bit is used to cut "V"- shaped grooves that lie parallel and in uniform proximity to best emulate the barbules on a feather.

Single stroke texturing is accomplished by using single strokes of the bit to cut the texture lines (barbules), each running in the same direction by starting at the top or bottom of the feather and applying single strokes side by side across the surface of the feather.

Double stroke texturing is accomplished by cutting the texture lines on the forward stroke as well as the backward stroke in a miniscule zigzag pattern across the surface of the feather.

While texturing, endeavor to follow your flow lines while curving the strokes slightly from side to side to imitate the pattern of the barbules on a contour feather – cause your strokes to curve in-ward slightly on either side with a few fairly straight strokes somewhere near the middle to transition to the change of direction.

To achieve a natural look of the feathers lying one over the other, two **major** rules usually apply to accurate and realistic texturing – a) always texture from the rear and work forward and b) texture from the bottom feather and work up. As you texture a feather that lies above a feather you have already textured, occasionally allow a stroke that is in line with the strokes on the finished feather below, to drift down over the completed feather. This gives an unobtrusive "flow" to the feathers by tying them together.

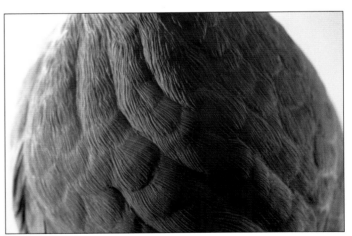

Feather Outlining with a Bent Tip Burner

1. Draw the flight feather groups to be textured with woodburning in place with a pencil. For symmetry, use care to insure that feathers match from side to side in shape, size, and number.

2. Begin outlining individual feathers using the bent tip outlining pen. This tip was designed specifically for this operation – the skewed end after the bend allows you to run the blunted straight edge of the skew along a drawn feather line, leaving an indented outlined feather edge that perfectly represents a feather as it lies on a bird.

First, test/adjust the heat setting for the pen by using it on a similar piece of wood as the wood that was used for the carving. This will save the carving from any initial burning errors caused by having the heat setting too high. On Tupelo, I try to attain a nice milk chocolate burn setting that allows the pen to move with as little friction as possible and without heavy charring if I hesitate.

3. Outline any exposed quills after all the feathers within a group have been outlined. If you feel insecure about burning the quills in accurately, practice on a piece of test wood first. Being right handed, I find it easier to "line-in" the left side of a quill first, then the right side – allowing me to more accurately taper the quill gradually and nicely to a point before the feather end.

Feather Texturing with a Skew Tip Burner

As with the feather outlining operation, insure that your skewed woodburning tip is set at a comfortable and appropriate heat setting for you to burn the line representing barbules on your feathers.

As you texture, if the pen stroke offers no resistance, chances are your heat setting is too high and will result in a stroke that is too deeply burned. If your heat setting is too cool, the resultant stroke will not only be too shallow, but after a time, the process will cause hand/finger fatigue due to the amount of pressure being exerted to achieve the desired effect and depth.

Keep the texturing strokes as close together as possible to accomplish the best and most natural looking effect. Too often we have a tendency to hurry, and in our haste, the appearance and quality of the texturing process suffers. If the strokes of your texturing were viewed in cross-section, it should look like an even row of "V"s, not like a row of randomly placed "V"s missing every few strokes, creating voids or flats between the barbules being represented.

Correct

Incorrect

Setting Eyes

Note: Every project in this book is scaled to accept brown colored 4 or 5mm eyes. These eyes are obtainable through any woodcarving suppliers or taxadermy supply houses.

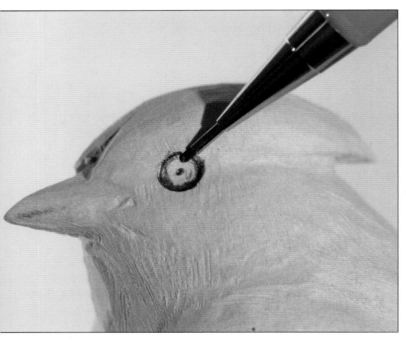

☐ I used a +3/16-inch ruby ball to create the eye cavities on every carving in this book. To carve the eye cavity, set the ball bit exactly on the center of the eye location and, while applying a downward pressure, begin a circular motion until the depth and width of the cavity is achieved. *Note: Put the eyes in a plastic bag and fit them to the cavity until they barely slide into the cavity opening – this will insure that enough space has been left to push the eye into the cavity once the bedding material has been put into the cavity.*

☐ Locate the exact location of each eye, insuring that they are not only properly located with respect to distance from the bill and the top/bottom of the head, but that the locations agree with one another from side to side when viewed from the top and front.

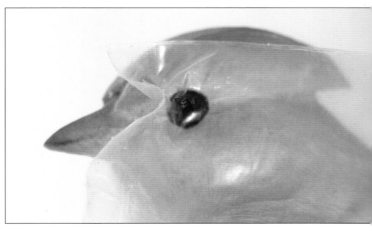

☐ Once the eye cavities are relieved, stone texturing around the eyes can be accomplished at any time during the contour feather texturing with a stone. Do not set the eyes until texturing is completed in the area of the eyes. The slightest touch of a rotating texturing stone on a glass eye will scar the glass surface and consequently ruin the appearance of the carving.

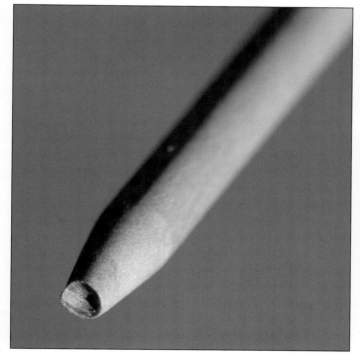

☐ Make a modeling tool from a 6 or 7 inch length of 1/4-inch birch dowel with a tapered edge at one end for modeling and material removal, such as the Avocet head shown with eyelids being modeled. Use a pencil sharpener and a ball bit to taper and establish a concave tip at the opposite end of the modeling tool. A concave end is necessary for holding against the eye and exerting pressure as the eye is pushed/directed into place within the material filled eye cavity. *Note the excess bedding material has filled the textured area outside and around the eyelids in the Avocet eyelid photo (I used a larger bird for clarity). To remove this excess, just turn the modeling tool wedge on the side and swipe in the textured grooves that are filled. This swiping motion not only cleans the textured grooves, but will allow additional texture lines to be added if necessary.*

☐ Fill the cavity with eye setting compound. Note: Depending on the size of the eye, I use a combination of 5-minute and 20-minute Quickwood® (an A + B type of epoxy putty). For example, for eyes with a 12-millimeter diameter and below, I use the 5-minute material not only to bed the eye, but to model the eyelids from the excess material that squeezes out around the eye as it is set to the proper depth. If the eye is over 12 millimeters in diameter, such as an owl eye of 20mm, I bed the eyes with 5 minute material, allow it to set, then form a small rope of material around the eye edges with 20 minute material and model the larger eyelids carefully and without rushing, given the longer setting time the material provides.

☐ Push the eye into the bedding material using the concave indentation on the end of the modeling tool. Control the depth and plumbness of the eye by applying necessary pressure with the modeling tool. If you bed the eye too deeply, pull it out and start again before the bedding material sets up, otherwise you will have to grind the eye out using a diamond bit or a steel bit.

The excess material that squeezes out around the eye can be used to model the eyelid if done within the time allowed by the setting bedding material. If you fall behind, quickly clean off the excess, and model the eyelids by applying a string of material around the eye as mentioned above. Make a string of material slightly larger than the finished eyelids that you need by rolling a ball of material back and forth between your fingers until it comes to an appropriate size.

☐ Model the eyelids to the appropriate configuration of the bird you are carving and allow them to set up completely before cleanup. You will note a film over the surface of the eye as a residual from the bedding material… Do not worry about it until the bedding has set up completely, then just rub the exposed surface of the eye with the moistened end of your modeling stick and the eye surface will clean to a nice normal shine.

Carving Eyes

If you choose not to install glass eyes, a very simple but effective method is to carve the eye using a very small flame shaped diamond bit with a fine grit in the following manner:

☐ Locate the exact center of both eyes with a penciled dot – make sure they are located symmetrically from side to side when viewed from the front and from the top of the carving.

☐ Carefully draw the circular outline of the eye to the finished size you want the eye to be. Again, insuring that the circles match from side to side.
☐ With a small diamond flame shaped bit, and holding the handpiece in a high position, carefully outline the **outside** of the eye circles until you attain the depth that readily represents a natural eye.

☐ Round the exposed circular shape as closely as possible to a uniform domed shape, dress edges as necessary, and this kinglet's eye is complete.
☐ To paint the eye, cover it entirely with the eye color of the bird you are carving (in the case of this kinglet, I would cover the entire eye with a burnt sienna/burnt umber combination to get a nice medium brown) – for the pupil, put a dot of black right in the middle of the eye by touching the end of a small brush handle in a puddle of black paint on your palette and with a light "touch and off" motion you can leave a perfect circle in the center of the eye. On smaller eyes, a toothpick works just as well. No matter what the size of the pupil is, just make sure you repeat the operation in the same manner, in the same location, with the same amount of paint for the second eye.

Red-breasted Nuthatch Working Drawing

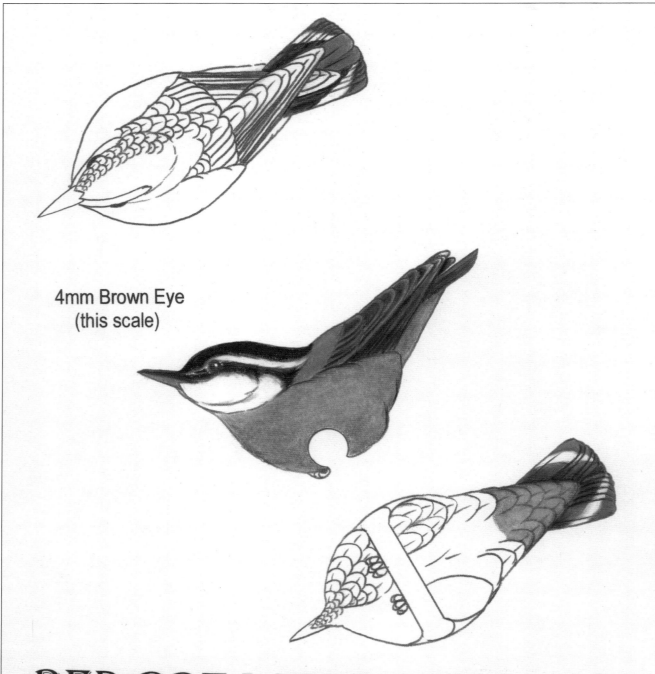

4mm Brown Eye
(this scale)

RED-BREASTED NUTHATCH

© 2004

Carving the Nuthatch

1. Select a carving block that is light (in weight) and has a close grain that will readily accept carving detail. For a carving that is to be painted, such as all the carvings in this book, I used Tupelo. I have also used basswood and poplar. Rarely do I use an unpainted surface for this type of carving – they don't show up as well as the colored birds on a tree, wreath, table setting, or wherever else they are placed. Where carvings like these are to be used as ornaments in settings such as a Christmas tree, I make my texturing lines a little coarser than I normally would to create more shadow when the lights of the tree shine across them. Given the location and the color of the bird, I feel the heavier quality of texture on the bird is more attractive.

2. Create top and side view templates by gluing copies of the pattern views to poster board or thick manila folder material. Cut around the outline of each view with a razor knife (which usually works better than scissors) ensuring that each of the templates is of equal length so that the blank will be accurately cut.

3. Draw each pattern outline on the carving block. The block should have at least a quarter inch waste area on the top and bottom of the side view, and the sides of the top view for safer, more comfortable, and accurate cutting on a band saw.

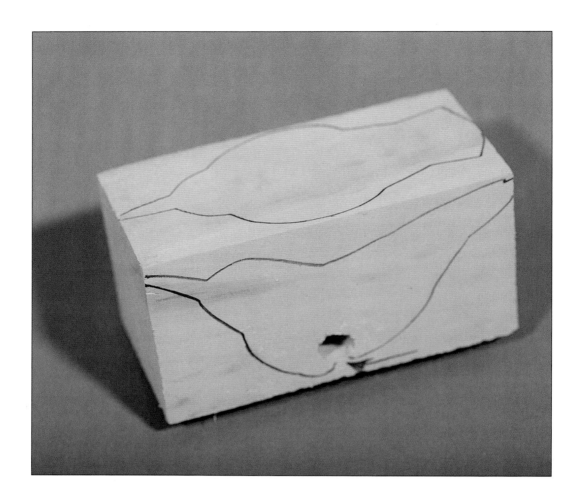

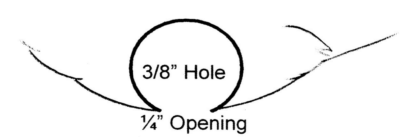

3/8" Hole

¼" Opening

4. While the block is still in its squared condition, drill a 3/8-inch hole all the way through the block located as shown on the working drawings and pattern. This hole will allow the carving to "perch" on the limb of an evergreen tree in a realistic manner.

5. Cut the side view first, as it usually offers more outline detail to deal with, such as shape of the beak, wing separations, and tail detail. Plan the cuts so that the entire top results in one piece and the entire bottom results in one piece. This is necessary for the next step.

6. Reassemble the three cut pieces and wrap securely with one or two turns of masking tape in the middle of the block. The portion of the pattern to be cut that the tape lies over should be visible through the tape, but if not, re-establish the hidden lines under the tape by drawing around the top view template again.

7. Cut the top view by cutting from one end or the other into the tape portion, then starting from the other end, finish the side cut by guiding the saw blade into the existing kerf (cut made by the saw blade).

8. Examine the sawn blank for accuracy of cut, and any granular flaws such as splits or checks.

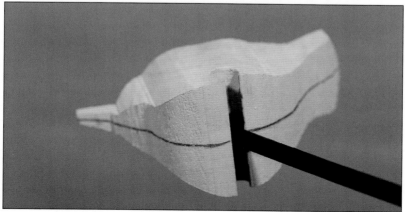

9. Draw a centerline around the entire bird from bill to tail.

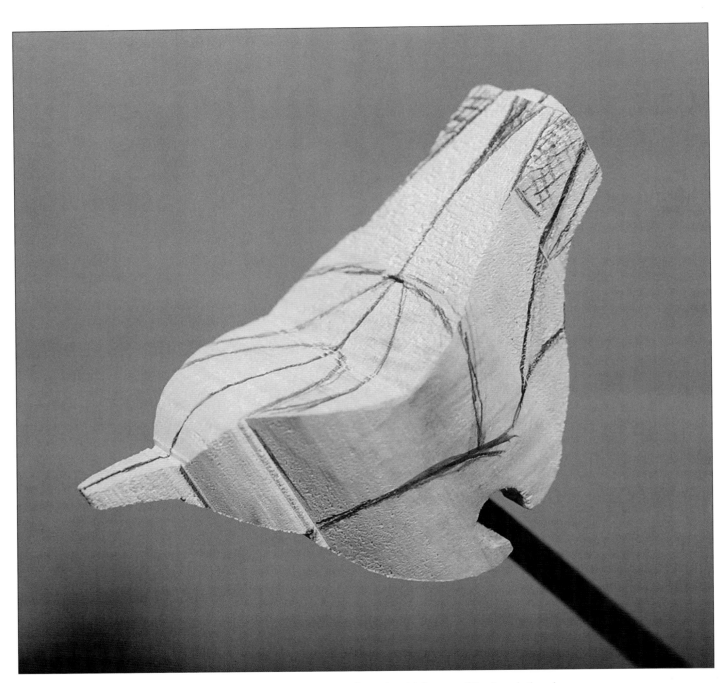

10. Layout extremes of major shapes to be relieved away such as the thickness of the head, the shape of the wings, the finished outline of the tail, and the mound where the feet will be unless the feet are to be covered by feathers.

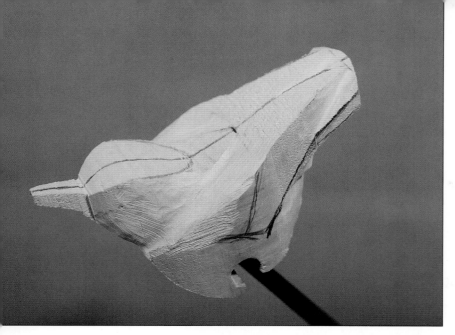

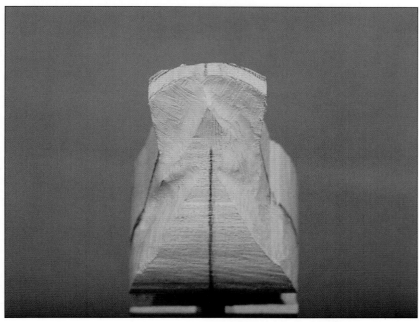

11. With a medium sized flame shaped carbide bit block out the major shapes of the bird.

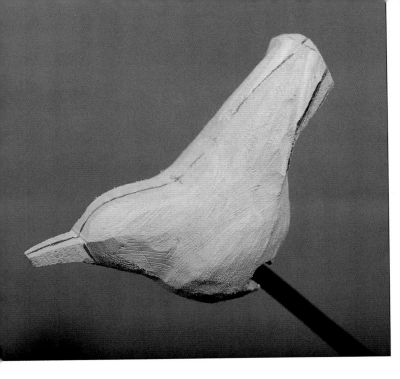

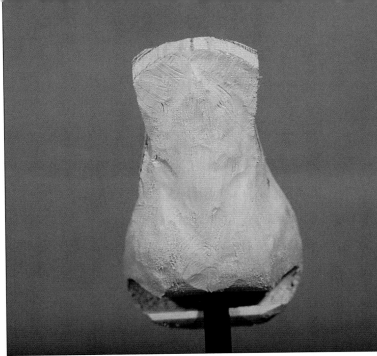

12. Round out all contours with a small carbide bit, then smooth and finish shape the major contours with a large flame shaped ruby carver.

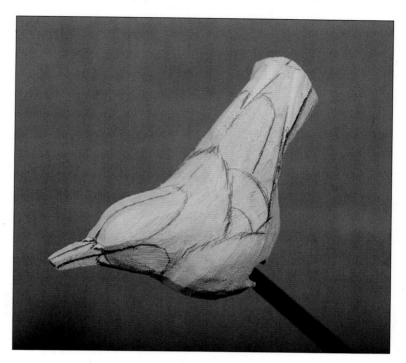

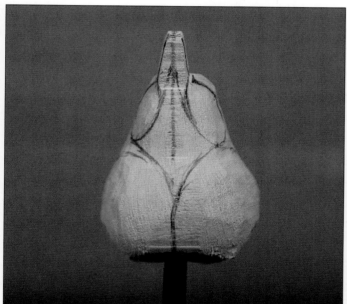

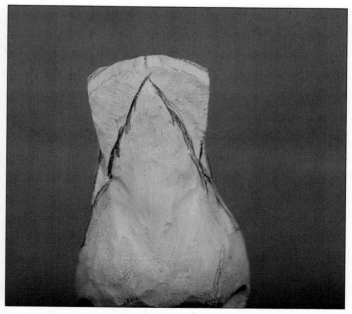

13. Pencil in the finished contoured areas of the bird – these will include feather groups, finished shape of the wings and tail, breast separations (if any), and the feet.

14. Round out and finish shape all the areas addressed in the previous step as necessary with a large or small flame shaped ruby carver.

15. At this point I locate the eyes. If I plan to carve the eye, I cut it in with the tip of a small flame shaped diamond or ruby carver bit. If I plan to install glass eyes, I locate and finish contour the eye cavities. I want the depth for the eyes, shape of the eye "valleys", and all contours surrounding the eyes to be equal and symmetrical from side to side before I apply the finish texturing that surrounds the eyes. See "Setting Eyes" as previously sequenced in this book.

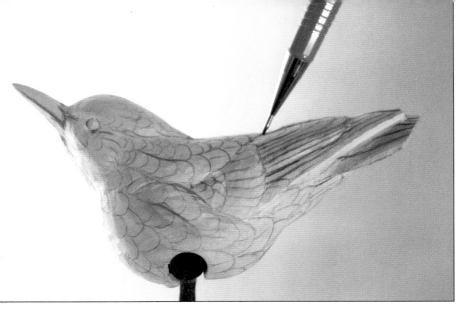

16. Draw feather detail over the entire bird. Give attention to the size of feathers drawn to insure that they are of a scale that matches the size of the bird. Hold the carving at arm's length and ascertain that the feathers are not only of correct size, but of correct shape for the species being carved.

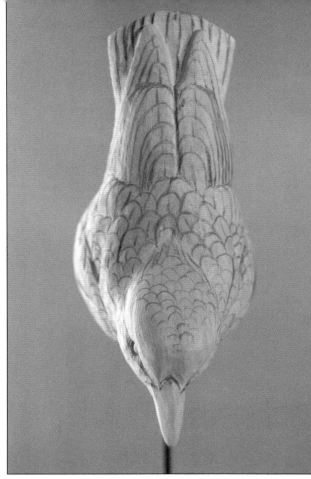

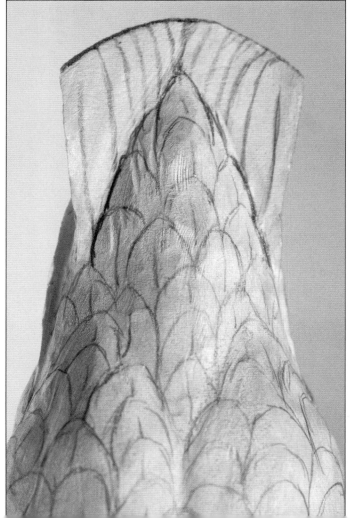

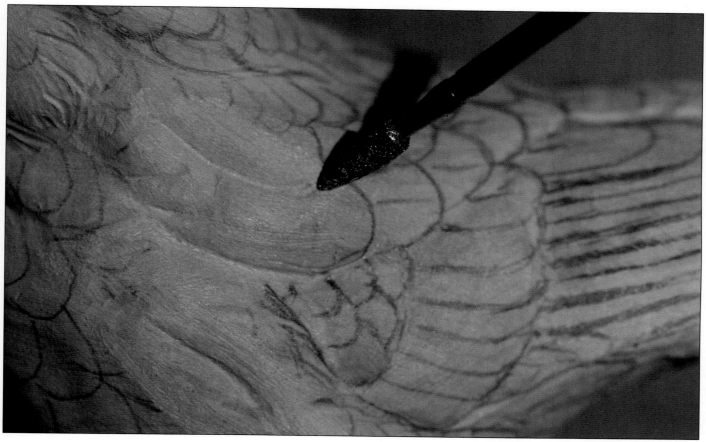

17. Since all of these birds will be placed on a perch, I want them to have that relaxed, "puffy" look that birds assume when they are at rest on a perch or roost. To help achieve this look, while I am drawing the contour feathers on the sides, chest, and cape, I draw a heavy line where several feathers lay pretty much side by side to give me an idea where I want the feather "bunches" to appear. If I like what I see, I use a small flame shaped ruby carver to cut a fairly deep groove along the line (which will serve as a separation space), then blend back into existing feathers. I redraw the feather lines in preparation for the feather outlining step. Caution: It is not necessary to over-do these separations.

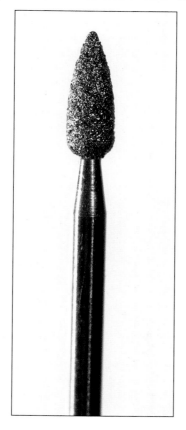

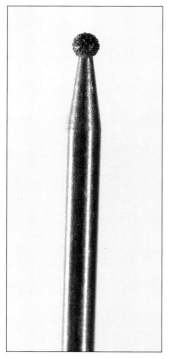

18. With a 1/32-inch diamond ball bit, outline all the contour feathers, this will include the head, chest, cape, sides, flanks, and undertail.

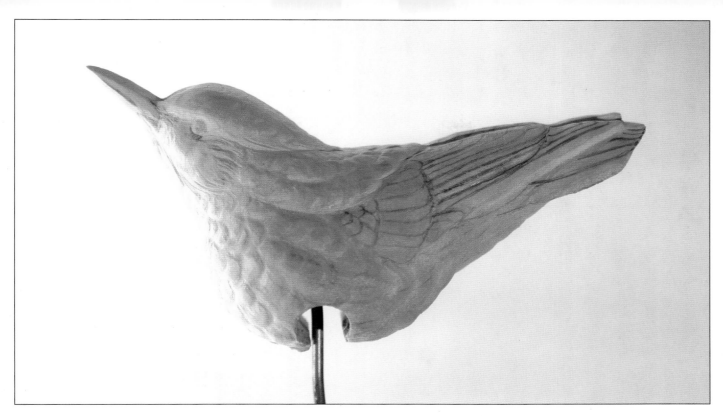

19. Using a fluted, tapered steel bit or a flame shaped stone bit, relieve away and finish shape all contour feathers over the entire carving.

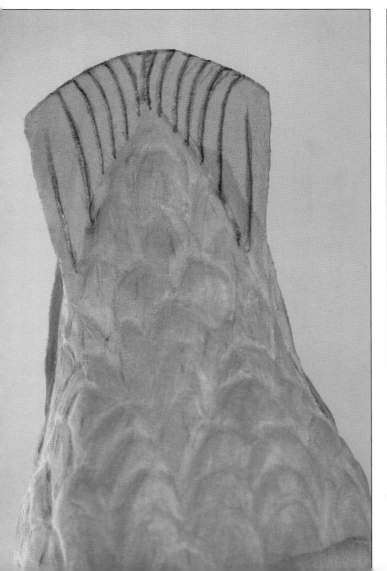

20. With a bent blade outliner woodburning pen, outline all flight feathers. This will include primaries, secondaries, tertials, alula, greater/median wing coverts, tail feathers, and any other feathers you may want to highlight or accentuate.

 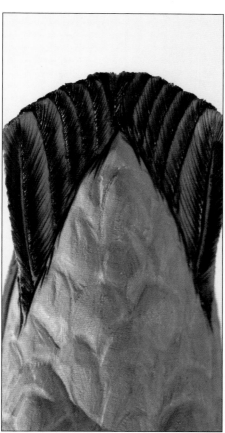 

21. Texture all flight feathers with a skew woodburning pen.

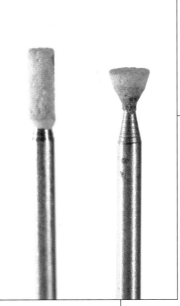

22. Texture all contour feathers with a cylinder shaped or an inverted cone shaped stone.
23. Set glass eyes or carve them as demonstrated earlier in this book

24. Clean the entire carving with a rotary brush. It is imperative that the carving be free of any dust particles or debris associated with the texturing process.

Preparation Prior to Painting

Color Matching

Before you begin the painting sequence, surround yourself with color photo references and/or any other pictorial references with color schemes or schematics that you prefer. If you **have** a proven color scheme (such as one you or someone else has used before and you know to be fairly accurate), select the colors and/or color mixes you will need and set them in a convenient place at your painting station ready for use. I do this because I dislike rummaging through my paint box looking for a color or colors I need to continue painting, when I should have had my colors chosen and prepared before I started painting.

If you **don't have** a proven color scheme, you should take the time to mix and match colors against a good colored source of the subject bird, such as a study skin, a fresh taxidermy mount, and/or your collection of colored reference photos. When I begin mixing colors for a carving against my collection of color photos, I find that shades of the same color vary because of a combination of things that have affected the finished photo, such as clarity, focus, light, type of photo paper used, and even the method used for photo processing. When I encounter a situation such as this, I take what I consider to be the one best representative color from all the references I have, or, as a last ditch effort, I take the best average of all the shades of the same color in my photos and use it.

Note: You will find that you have a greater range of color shades than you suspect, so make the choice of color(s) that best satisfies **you** *and* your reference collection. I was amazed at the variance of the color red on a tray of male cardinal study skins at one museum I visited. I have found the same variances in every collection of bird study skins that I have had the opportunity to observe.

Once the paint schedule is prepared and the paints arranged and ready, I give attention to setting up my position with regard to paint application.

My usual method to apply paint to any carving is through a combination of airbrushing and manual brushing, so with this in mind, I set up my painting station in such a manner that all accessories are ready and within easy reach.

Painting Equipment and Accessories

My checklist for airbrushing and manual paint application, consists of the following accessories:

☐ Airbrush, hose, and hanger
☐ Compressor (or **any** continuous source of clean, dry air)
☐ Assortment of brush sizes (Filberts & Rounds)
☐ Clear Acrylic Lacquers (**flat** for sealing and **glossy** for beaks, feet, and carved eyes)
☐ Gesso (for surface preparation)
☐ Acrylic paints (both tube and air brush preparations)
☐ Paint extender and/or retarder
☐ Glass plate paint palette (I use a thick piece of glass 10" x 10" or larger) with the underside painted white or laid on a white paper towel) – I find the whitened neutral surface showing through helps me to mix paint color more accurately.
☐ Several small mixing trays
☐ Two water tubs (usually motel ice buckets)
☐ Filtered waste tub (used to check or clear the airbrush after changing colors or cleaning) – I stretch about three layers of cheesecloth over a 2-quart plastic container, such as paint stores carry, and secure the cheesecloth firmly over the rim of the container with a heavy rubber band such as mailmen carry to bundle letters in. The container is then filled half full of water, and whenever I need to test the spray, check the intensity of a color, or waste out airbrush cleaner, I hold the

nozzle fairly close to the cheesecloth and spray full force into the container, which arrests all of the spray particles.

☐ Airbrush cleaner (usually Windex® window cleaner)

☐ Paper towels

☐ Hair dryer

Everything suggested above, as preparation for painting the nuthatch, applies to **any** carving you want to paint, whether it is a bird, animal, or human.

Holding Handle and Base

Years ago I learned that the best way to paint a carving was to keep my hands off the carving entirely. I used oil paints on the first decorative birds

I painted and the oils took so long to dry that the choice was either to wait for each application to dry (which took days unless I used Japan dryer) or devise a holding handle of some sort that would allow a completely hands off method to paint the carvings. I finally settled on the holding sticks and base shown here that allows me to hold the carving steady and securely in any position while I paint it.

I have used acrylic paints for many years now, and wouldn't be without the holding handles for any songbird that I paint. By holding a carving with your bare hands as you paint, the movement of your hand on the carving coupled with the moisture from your palm will give the painted surface a shiny, plastic, unnatural look by the time you have finished painting. Some carvers I know who prefer to hold a carving as they paint it, wear lightweight cotton gloves to alleviate any possibility of shine or glossing.

The handle is simply made – a 1/2-inch birch dowel cut to a suitable length (6 to 8 inches), with a hole drilled in one end to accept a coarse 1 1/2-inch sheet rock screw. The head is nipped off the screw with a heavy set of lineman pliers and a hole to fit the screw is drilled about 7/8-inch deep in the end of the dowel. After fitting the headless screw to the hole (there should be 5/8-inch of the screw sticking out of the dowel) sharpen the hole end of the dowel using a sander leaving a slight shoulder of stock around the hole. Fill the hole nearly full with 5-minute epoxy using a toothpick and twist the screw in the direction of the threads down into the hole. Wipe off excess epoxy and put aside until the epoxy sets up. I always make several to have on hand if I plan to paint more than one carving at a time.

The base has a hole that the handle is set in to keep the carving upright while mixing or preparing paint, cleaning brushes or an airbrush, drying with a hair dryer, or going to lunch. The base can be made from any scrap stock thick enough to accept a hole deep enough to hold the handle upright and wide/long enough to support and prevent a carving from toppling.

Screw the handle into an unobtrusive area of the carving such as inside the limb groove (see the patterns in this book), or where a leg will be placed on a regular bird carving. If not, you will have to fill and retexture the hole in the exposed area where the handle screw made a hole.

A "Lazy Susan" is another way to keep from handling the carving as you paint it. The piece being painted can be controlled directionally by turning and holding the upper layer of the turntable with your free hand. This method works well for animal carvings as well as larger bird carvings such as waterfowl. I made mine with two circles of 3/4-inch plywood and a small Lazy Susan fixture available at any hardware store. I prefer circles with a 12" upper platform and an 8" base.

Surface Preparation

Before applying color, the carving surface should first be prepared by sealing to close up cellular/grain structure to prevent possible checking and provide a uniform base on which to apply color. Secondly, the sealed surface requires an opaque layer of Gesso to prepare the entire surface to accept paint (much in the same way that a canvas is sized to accept paint).

Sealing

Seal the carving with a quality satin or flat clear acrylic lacquer. My preference is clear automotive acrylic lacquer, (available at most automotive supply stores). It is pricey, but it gives the very best results for sealing and surface conditioning – and a quart or pint goes a long way.

A second choice, if automotive acrylic lacquer is unavailable, is a quality polyurethane satin finish – one brand name that I use quite often is Deft© satin finish polyurethane finish.

Whether an acrylic lacquer or poly finish, I thin with lacquer thinner using a 50/50 mixture of lacquer to thinner, and after a careful final examination* of the carving, I apply anywhere from 3 to 5 coats of the thinned lacquer mixture to the entire carving using a hair dryer to dry between each coat. Permit the carving to accept all the sealing mixture that the granular structure of the wood will allow to insure total and deep penetration.

Using a 1/2-inch flat soft bristle brush "flow" the lacquer mixture onto the carving, spreading what the brush has carried, then stroke the emptied brush over what has been covered to clean any excess that has pooled in any detail depressions.

*Note: Before applying the lacquer sealer coats, visually inspect the carving for a final time to insure that all the detail you want is in/on the carving. Once the sealer coats have been applied, it is difficult to achieve additional detailing or corrections because of the thickness of the lacquer sealer coats – the correctional process will take additional time, and

at the very least, you will plug any of the finer power carving bits.

Applying Gesso

Obtain the finest "grained" Gesso you can find – the finer the gesso particle, the better. In a small bottle or the mixing depression on a palette, add water to a portion of gesso until it has the consistency of heavy cream.

For projects the size of the birds in this book, I use a medium sized hog bristle Filbert brush and "scrub" the gesso mixture into every surface and detail depression on the carving. I prefer a manual brush over an airbrush first, because I learned that way, and secondly, I believe manual brushing better controls any loss of detail. The objective is to build to an opaque white without losing any of the finer carving detail. This usually will take up to 3 or 4 coats of the thinned gesso.

The first coat is thin enough that the yellowish hue of the wood can be seen through the transparency of the gesso. Dry each coat thoroughly with a hairdryer until the carving is completely covered with an opaque white. Once it has been thoroughly dried, the carving is ready to apply color.

Color Application

Once you select the array of colors you plan to use, you must decide in what manner you want to apply color to the different areas on the bird. Where can I use the airbrush to best advantage? Where will manual brush application be best? What will be the easiest, yet most effective method for me? ... Etc. Obviously, if you have never used an airbrush, this is not the point to plan on using one.

As previously stated, I like to use a combination of airbrush and manual brushes when I paint my carvings, but sometimes I use only manual brushes just for the joy of it. Conversely, on larger animal and waterfowl carvings I get as much satisfaction from using an airbrush.

It is not my intention to attempt to teach or convert anyone to my painting method – I have found a self-taught method of painting that satisfies me, but can easily change if/when I find a new product or painting technique that I like better.

Whatever your decision or method, make it a relaxing and enjoyable process.

Airbrush

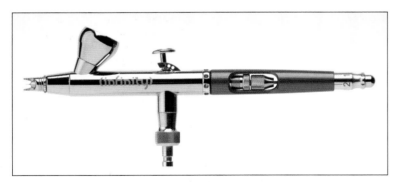

The airbrush that I used throughout this book is the Infinity manufactured in Germany by Harder & Steenbeck. This line of airbrushes and accessories is relatively new, having been introduced in the United States in August of 2007 (seven months prior to this writing). I found this particular model to be one of the easiest to adjust and operate, and as forgiving with respect to paint application as any I have ever used. It features an adjustable lever resistance, which is invaluable for customizing the airbrush to user preference. The Infinity "Quick Fix" feature consists of a knob with an engraved scale, which allows for greater paint-flow control, and the open needle cap ensures permanent control of the needle tip. Along with features previously listed, the Infinity carries a **10-year** warranty. Thanks to quality, craftsmanship, and versatility, the Infinity has become my primary use airbrush.

Manual Brushes

I only use two brush shapes, Rounds and Filberts, in several sizes depending on how I apply color and the size of the carving I am painting.

No matter the type of brush you use, buy the highest quality brush you can afford. The more expensive brushes cost more for a reason – they give the best result and if properly cared for will usually outlast the cheaper brushes.

The Filbert brushes are used for sealing, applying Gesso, base coat cover colors, and blending colors/transition zones.

To validate my findings on the Infinity, I allowed several of my students to "play" with it without suggestion or instruction to see what the results would be. Suffice to say, the results were significant enough for me to feature this airbrush as part of this book.

For a more complete description of this line of airbrushes and accessories, visit the company website at **www.germanairbrush.com** or write: *Harder & Steenbeck Airbrush, P.O. Box 10426, Brooksville, FL 34603 USA*

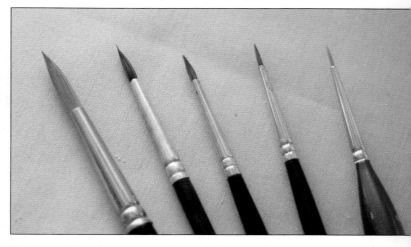

The Round brushes are used for painting detail and must have a very sharp point for lining along with a large barrel to hold a maximum amount of color. Kolinsky sable brushes compose the majority of rounds that I have. Depending on size, one of these brushes can cost as much as a meal out for two, but quality of use justifies (somewhat) the price. Two favorite makers of round brushes are Raphael® and Windsor-Newton® (Series 7).

The Painted Nuthatch

I painted the Nuthatch by blocking out the major color areas with an airbrush. These areas consisted of the russet blend for the chest, belly, flanks; the lighter white/cream colors on the bib, head, and under tail coverts; the blue-gray of the cape, back, and tail; and finally the black/raw umber head stripes. Everything else was painted using manual brushes – the primaries, tertials, tail feather detail, and softened areas of color transitions.

I used liquid acrylic airbrush colors for the entirety of the carving, which I thinned with water to apply in washes to attain the depth and shade of color that I wanted.

Final detailing such as the quills, feather splits, or additional feather detailing was done with a very small round brush.

To accentuate various areas that were too dark, or where I wanted to accentuate feather detail, I washed the designated area with a very thin wash (some call it antiquing) of a color suitable to enhance. Two examples of this method would be the thin wash of yellow ochre applied to the chest and belly to lighten and create a highlighted area, or the thin wash of raw umber on the bib, neck, and head to lightly accentuate the texturing.

Finishing Beaks, Eyes, and Feet

Once the carving is totally painted, I use a gloss acrylic lacquer to coat the beak to give it the hard glossy look that is normal to a real bird's beak. The same applies to the exposed toes and toenails.

If you have carved the eyes, and have them painted the color you want them, to give them a shiny "alive" look, coat them with one or more coats of gloss acrylic lacquer. Use care to cover just the dome shape of the eye and not the eyelids.

I use the smallest round brush that I have and apply lacquer around the outer eye first before covering the remainder of the eye. Allow each coat to dry thoroughly before applying an additional coat.

Dull Coating and Protective Finishing

There are times when an area you have painted is too shiny, either from handling too much or from using paint directly out of the tube or container. An extremely shiny surface isn't common to the appearance of a normal bird, so to alleviate extreme shininess, I use a clear "Dullcoat" spray by Testors® found in the plastic model paint section of hobby, department, or craft stores, or "Matte" clear spray by Krylon® found in art and paint stores.

In addition to reducing extreme shine, at least the very bottom of the ornament carving should be given a protective coat of the above mentioned products to protect the acrylic paint from being scratched or worn from repeated attachment to the branch of a Christmas tree, wreath, or other setting.

Attaching a Songbird Ornament

To attach your carved songbird ornament to a branch (specifically an evergreen), hold the end of the branch with your free hand for stability, and holding the ornament carving at a 45-degree angle away from you with the mounting hole aligned with the branch, push downward and roll the ornament into place on the branch, squeezing the branch and needles into the hole.

Working Drawings
and Carving Photos

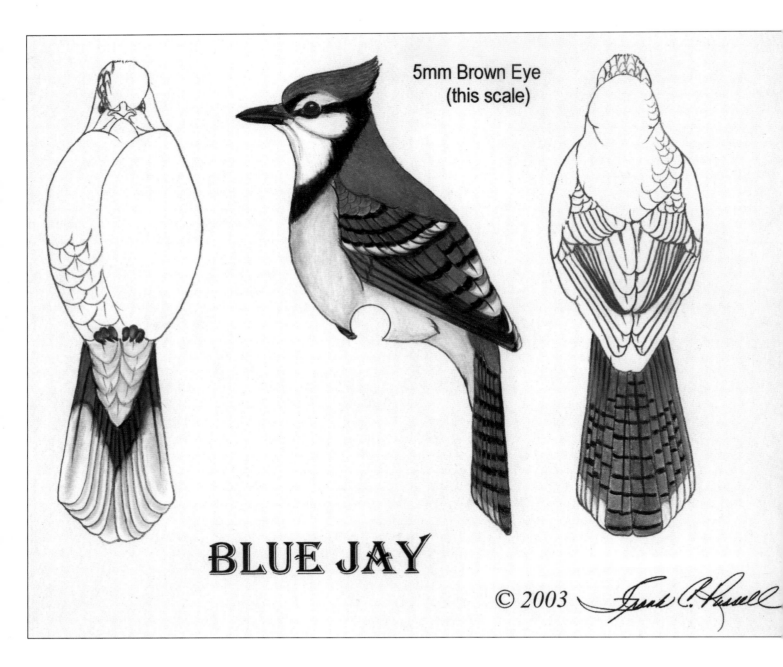

5mm Brown Eye
(this scale)

BLUE JAY

© 2003

Carved Bluejay

Carved Bluejay

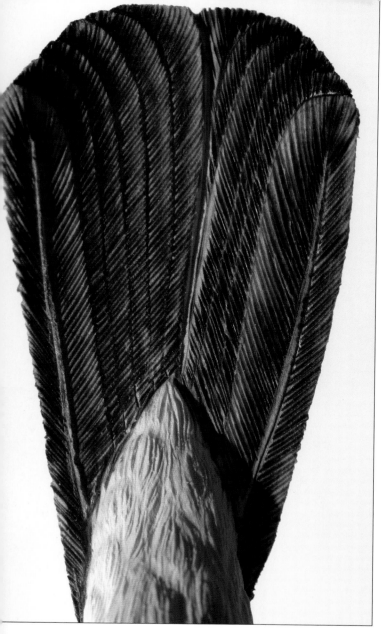

Carved Bluejay

Dropped Crest

5mm Dark Brown Eye
(this scale)

NORTHERN CARDINAL

© 2004

Carved Cardinal

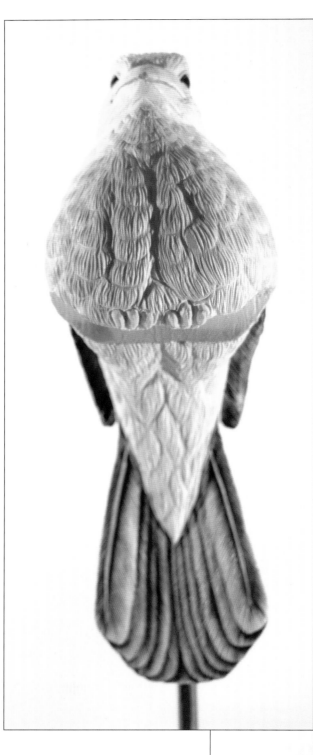

Carved Cardinal

Carved Cardinal

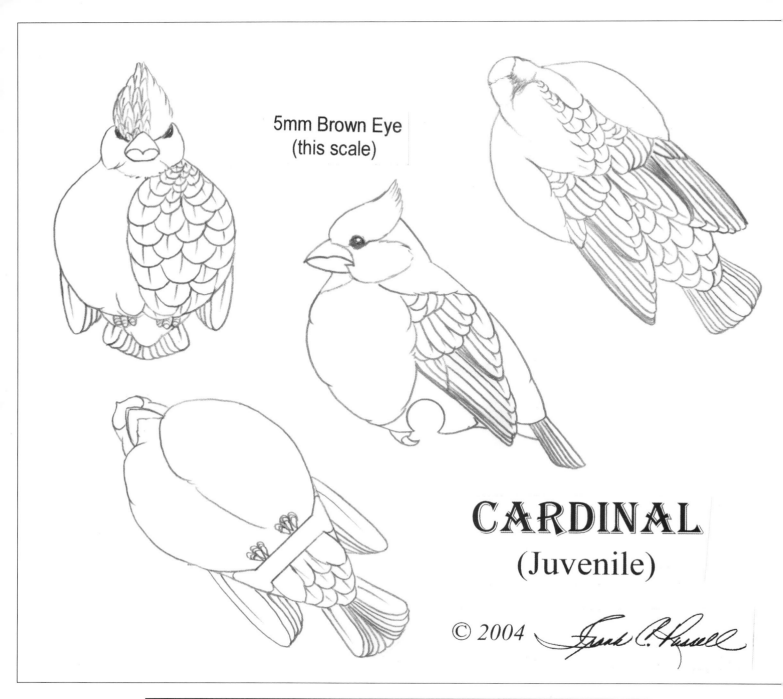

5mm Brown Eye
(this scale)

CARDINAL
(Juvenile)

© 2004

Carved Juvenile Cardinal

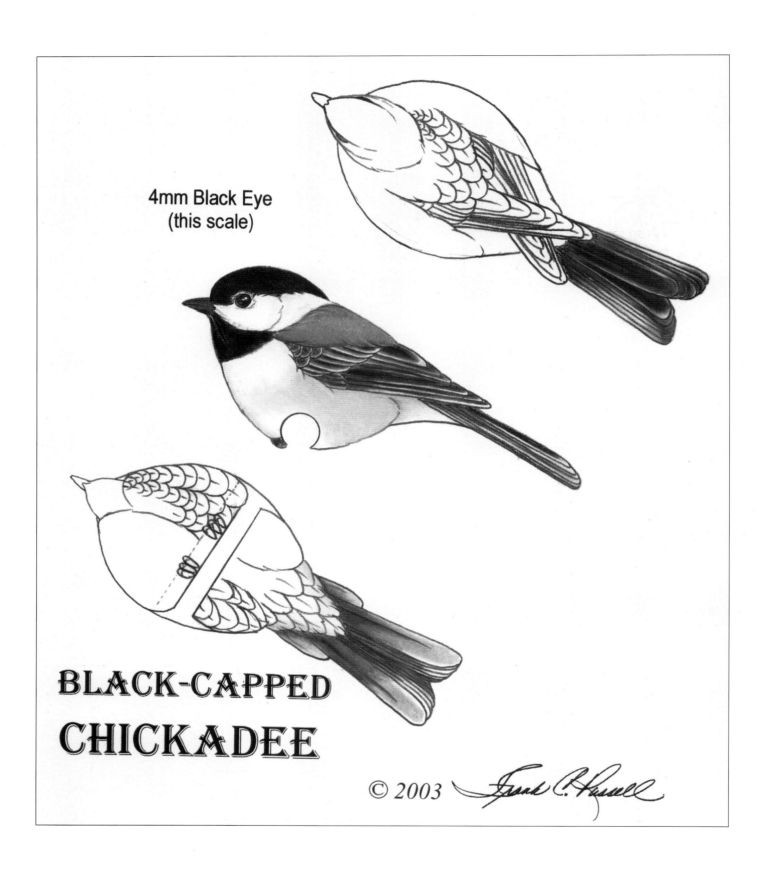

4mm Black Eye
(this scale)

BLACK-CAPPED CHICKADEE

Carved Chickadee

Carved Chickadee

Carved Chickadee

Top of Head

4mm Black Eye
(this scale)

TUFTED
TITMOUSE

© 2004

Carved Tufted Titmouse

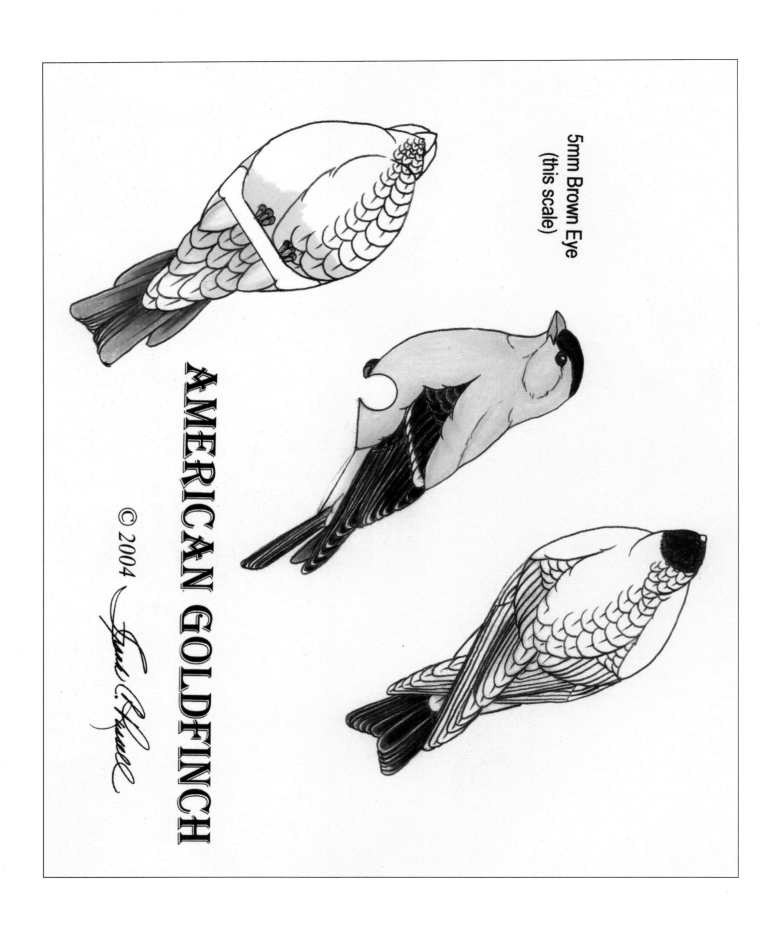

5mm Brown Eye
(this scale)

AMERICAN GOLDFINCH

© 2004

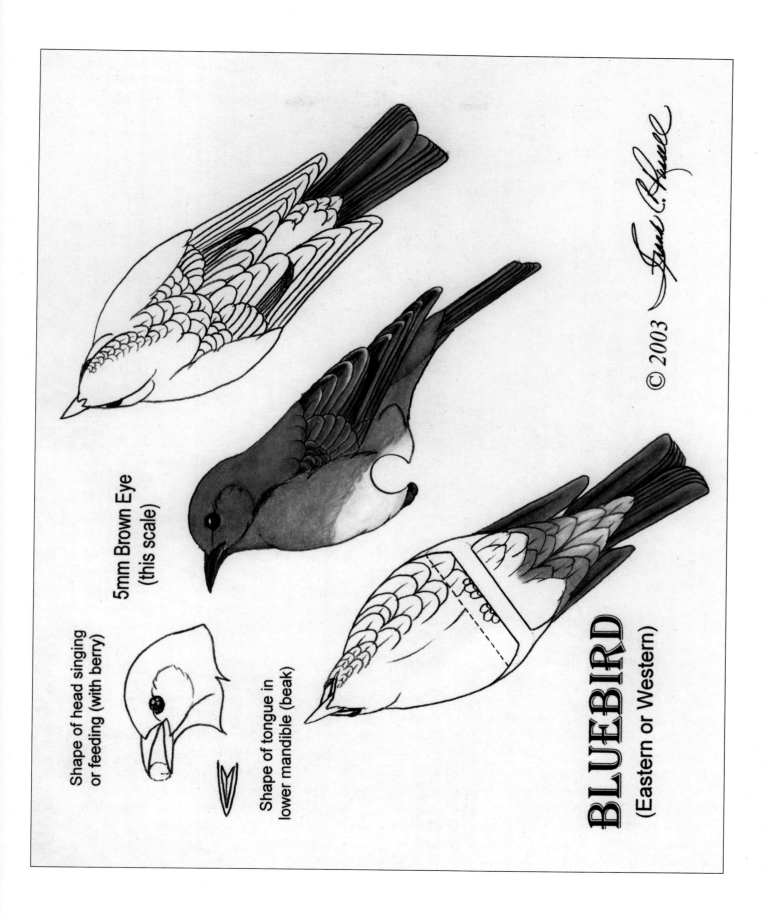

Shape of head singing
or feeding (with berry)

5mm Brown Eye
(this scale)

Shape of tongue in
lower mandible (beak)

BLUEBIRD
(Eastern or Western)

© 2003

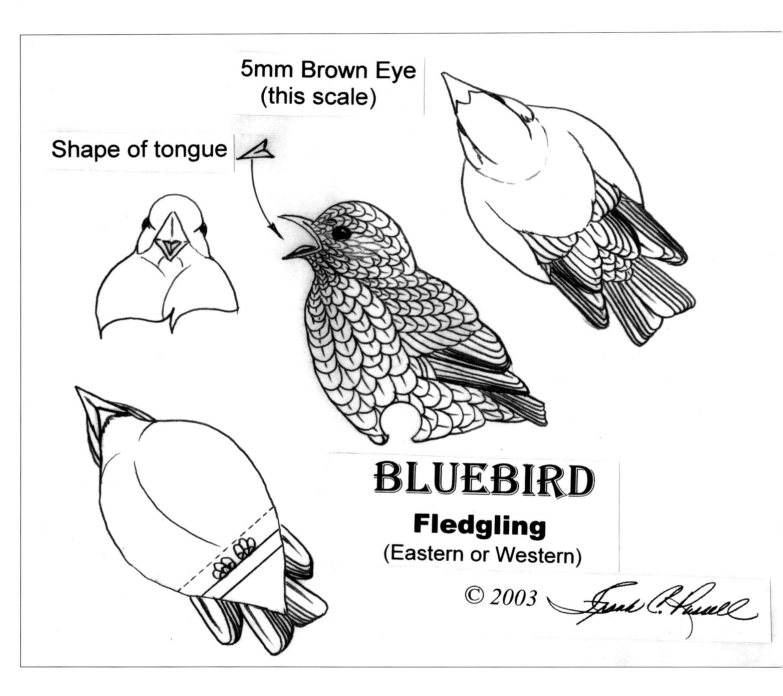

5mm Brown Eye
(this scale)

Shape of tongue

BLUEBIRD

Fledgling
(Eastern or Western)

© 2003

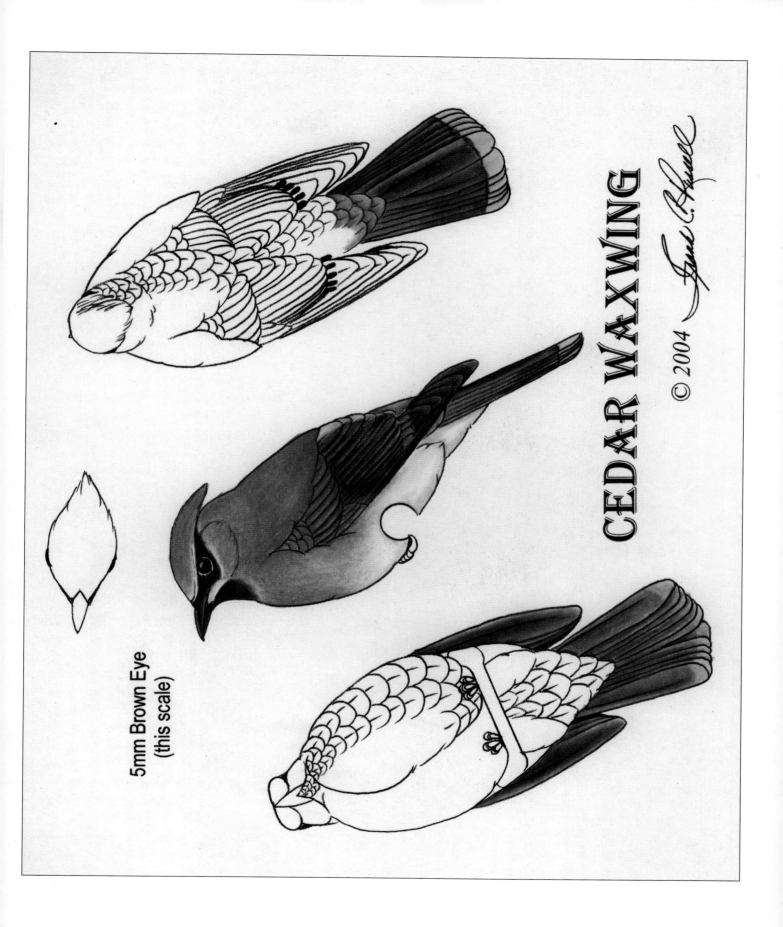

5mm Brown Eye
(this scale)

CEDAR WAXWING

© 2004

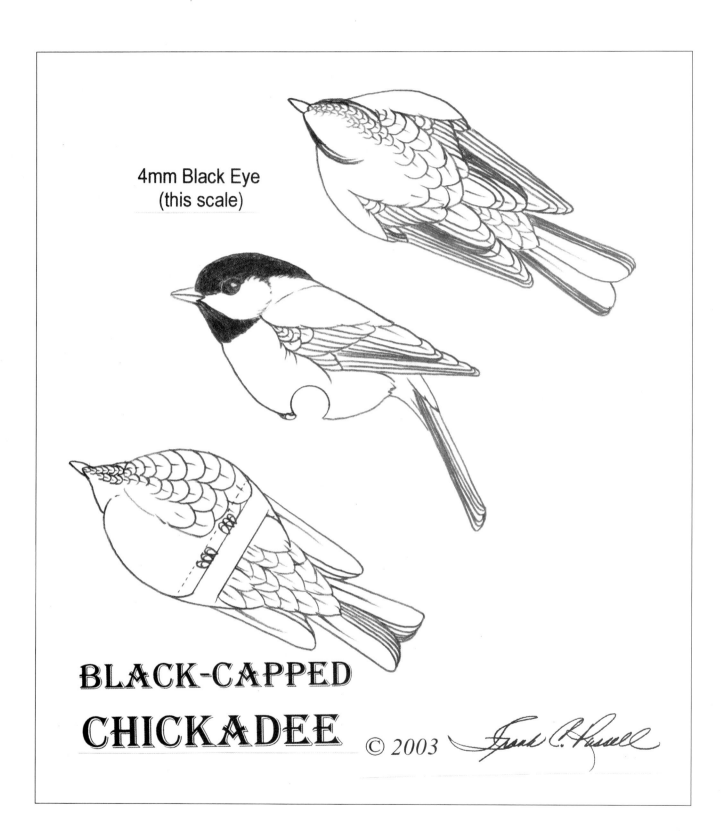

4mm Black Eye
(this scale)

BLACK-CAPPED
CHICKADEE
© 2003

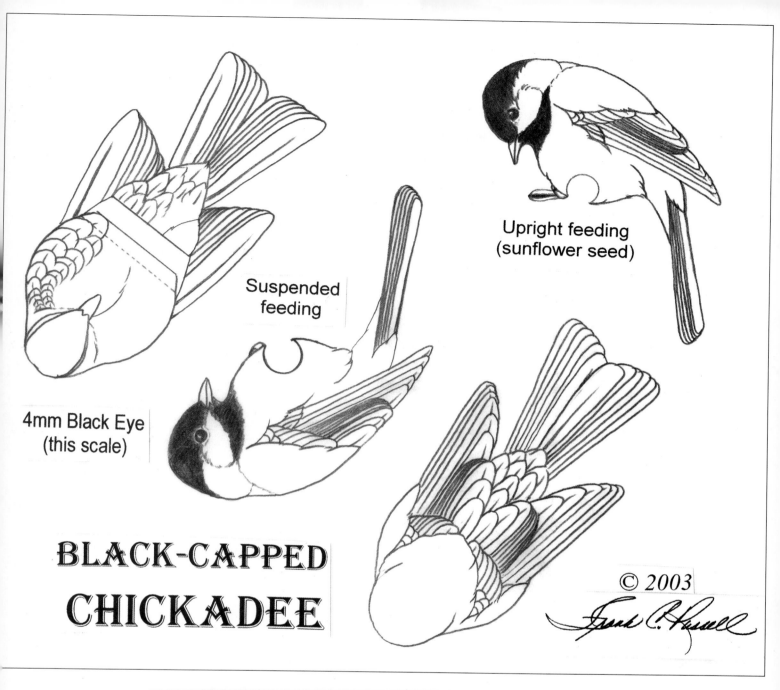

Upright feeding
(sunflower seed)

Suspended
feeding

4mm Black Eye
(this scale)

BLACK-CAPPED CHICKADEE

© 2003

BLACK-CAPPED CHICKADEE

Fledgling Feeding

4mm Black Eye
(this scale)

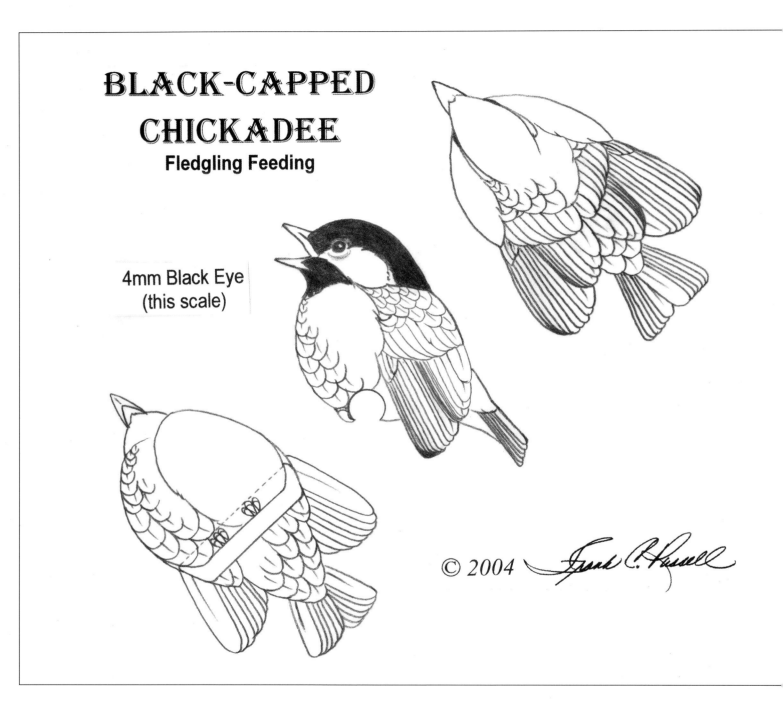

© 2004   *Frank C. Russell*

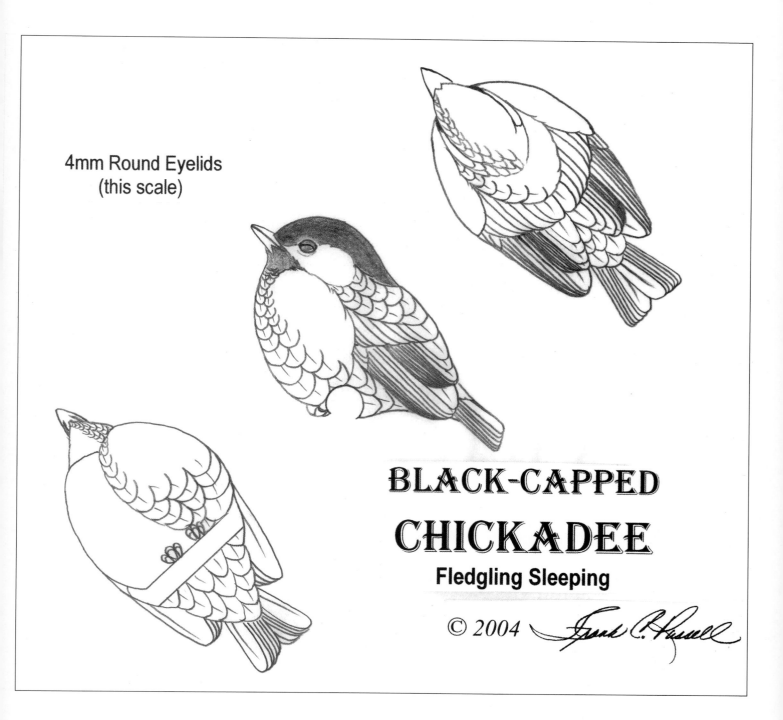

4mm Round Eyelids
(this scale)

BLACK-CAPPED
CHICKADEE
Fledgling Sleeping

© 2004

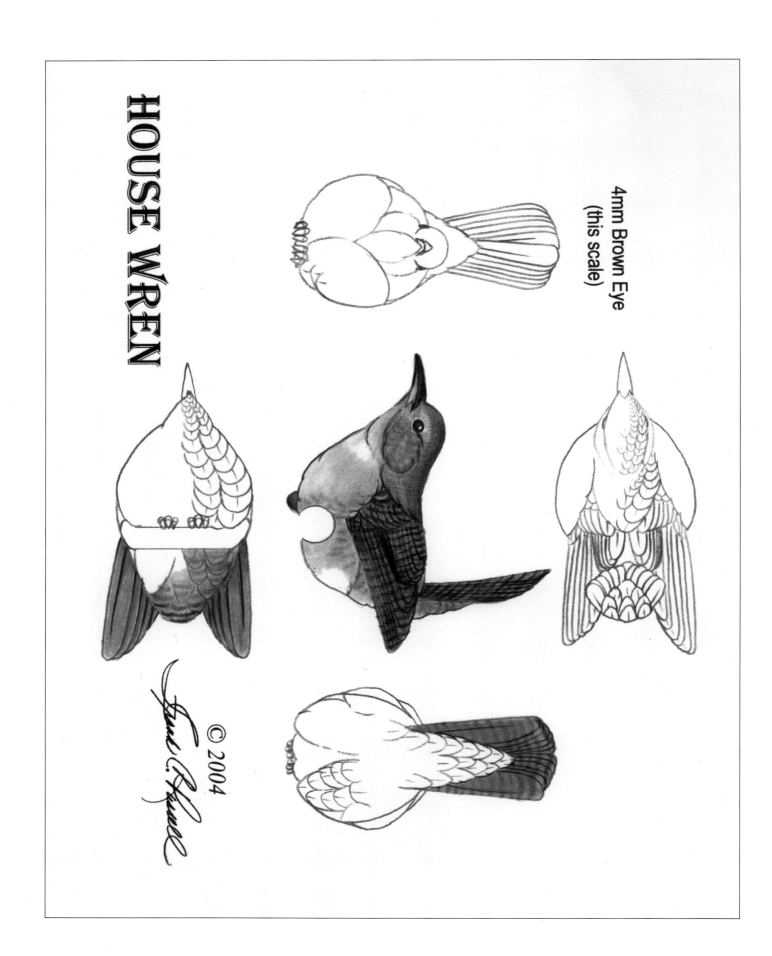

HOUSE WREN

4mm Brown Eye
(this scale)

© 2004

KINGLET

(Golden-crowned & Ruby Crowned)

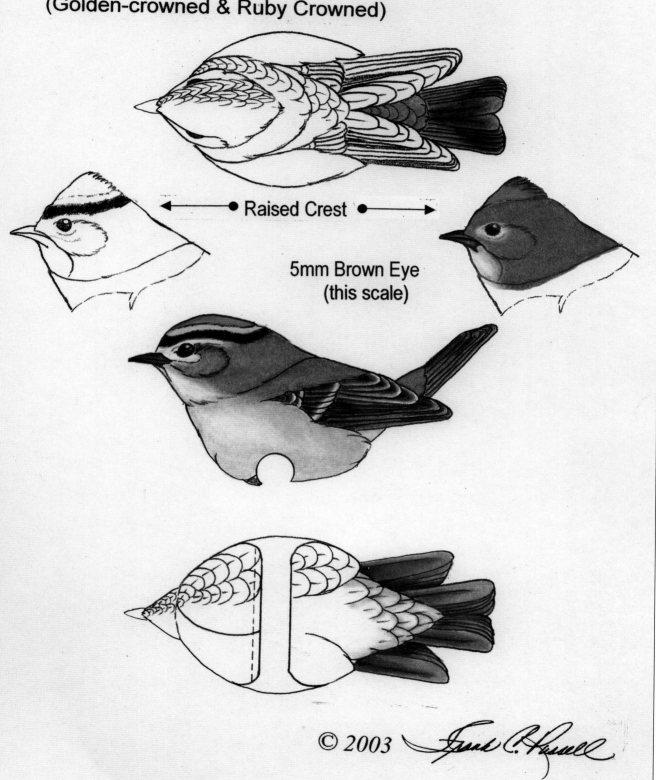

◆————— ● Raised Crest ● —————▶

5mm Brown Eye
(this scale)

© 2003

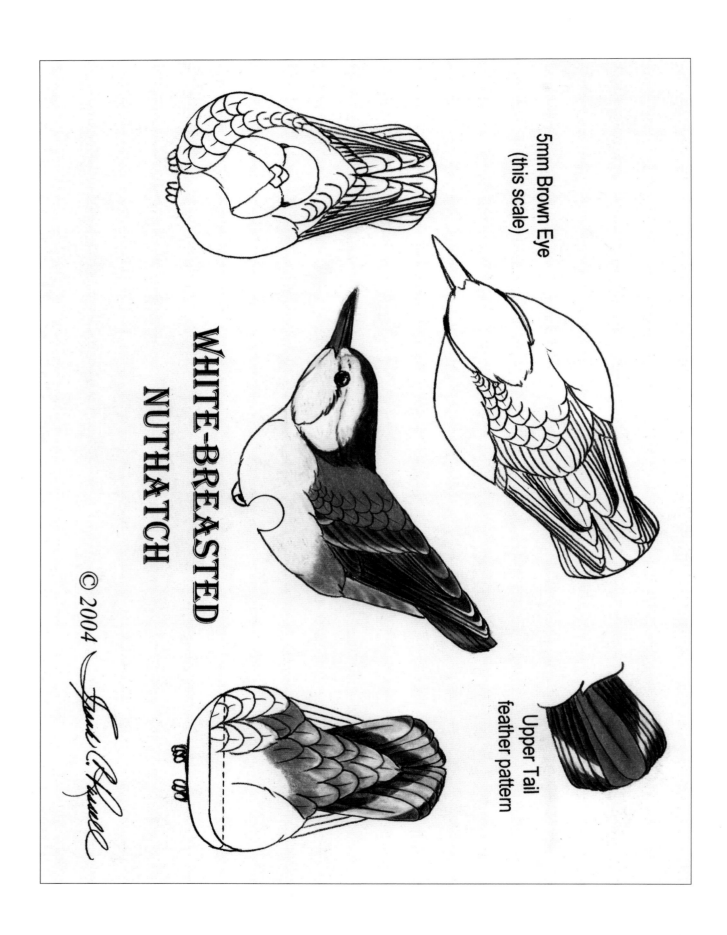

5mm Brown Eye
(this scale)

WHITE-BREASTED
NUTHATCH

© 2004

Upper Tail
feather pattern

78

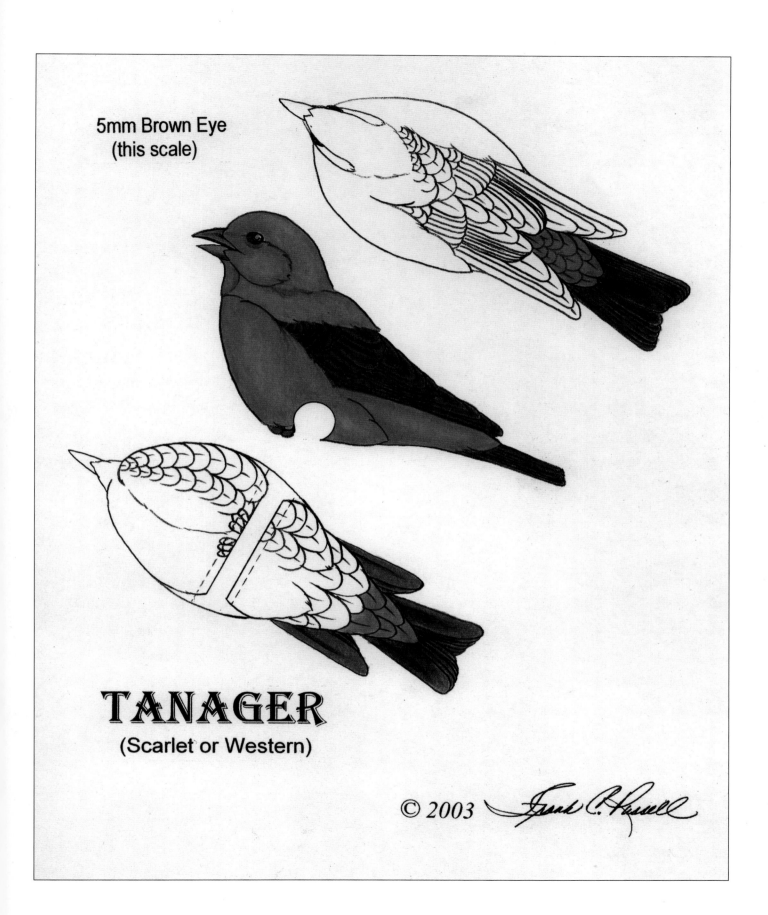

5mm Brown Eye
(this scale)

TANAGER

(Scarlet or Western)

© 2003

Top of Head

4mm Black Eye
(this scale)

TUFTED TITMOUSE

Juvenile

© 2004